Loving the Little Years

Loving the Little Years

MOTHERHOOD IN THE TRENCHES

Rachel Jankovic

canonpress
Moscow, Idaho

Published by Canon Press
P.O. Box 8729, Moscow, ID 83843
800.488.2034 | www.canonpress.com

Cover design by Rachel Hoffmann.
Interior design by Laura Storm.
Printed in the United States of America.

Library of Congress Cataloging-in-Publication Data

Jankovic, Rachel.
  Loving the little years : motherhood in the trenches / Rachel Jankovic.
    p. cm.
  ISBN-13: 978-1-59128-081-1 (pbk.)
  ISBN-10: 1-59128-081-8
  1. Mothers--Religious life. 2. Motherhood--Religious aspects--Christianity. 3. Child rearing--Religious aspects--Christianity. 4. Toddlers--Care. I. Title.
  BV4529.18.J37 2010
  248.8'431--dc22

                                        2010039484

13 14 15 16 17 18   14 13 12 11 10 9

To Luke
on whose shoulders we all ride

Contents

Foreword

Sometimes all we really need is a fresh perspective on our circumstances. We need someone to open a window and let a breeze blow into the room that we didn't realize had gotten so stuffy. This book is about opening the windows.

Mothers of little people have the most challenging and important job on earth. But it is a humble job. And it takes the eye of faith to see the fruit of a coming generation of faithfulness. This book is about hardship and humor, sacrifice and satisfaction.

Rachel Jankovic is a woman who lives out her story with humility, grace, and a houseful of humor. With five exuberant children, ages five and under, she knows what she is talking about. She keeps her windows open.

She called me just the other day when she was writing like crazy to meet the deadline for this book. Having been careful to not shortchange the kids while writing a book on loving them, she was squeezing her writing into the nooks and tight crannies of her days. On this particular day, she had opened the windows. The kids were wheeling around their small house, happily whooping it up while she was writing, and she was close to finishing. But a couple of flies had gotten into the house, much to her distraction.

"Mom," she said, "I need three things to make everything all right: a fly-swatter, a pumpkin candle, and a babysitter!"

I had to laugh! What a funny gift bag that would make (especially since Rachel isn't a big fan of scented candles). So, open the window, get out a fly-swatter, light a pumpkin candle, and sorry about the babysitter. I'm over at Rachel's.

Nancy Wilson

CHAPTER ONE

Welcome to My Circus

If there is anything I have learned in the course of my fast and furious mothering journey, it is that there is only one thing in my entire life that must be organized. The kids can be running like a bunch of hooligans through a house that appears to be at the bottom of a toaster, and yet, if organization and order can still be found in my attitude, we are doing well. But if my attitude falters, even in the midst of external order, so does everything else.

It is one thing to state this casually, another to believe it, and yet quite another to keep it in sight when you most need to. And if you have small children like I do, you need to keep it in mind all the time.

The following is a loose collection of thoughts on mothering young children—for when you are motivated, for when you are discouraged, for the times when discipline seems fruitless, and for when you are just plain old tired. Think of this as organizational tools for a mother's attitude. A lot of the time all you need is a good old perspective adjustment and a label.

This is not a tender reminiscence from someone who had children so long ago that she only remembers the sweet parts. I do not have a foggy, precious perspective on mothering little ones. My children do not sit on monogrammed picnic blankets in coordinated outfits while I bring them nutritious snacks on a silver tray. You are more likely to find me putting an end to them pulling each other around at breakneck speeds on a tablecloth tied to a jump rope, or seriously counseling someone who has part of a toilet paper tube taped to their nose. At the time of writing this, I have three children in diapers, and I can recognize the sound of hundreds of toothpicks being dumped out in the hall. Sure, I am looking back in retrospect on nursing the twins in the park with a blanket between my teeth, but it wasn't so long ago that I have forgotten about the overheated kind of specialness of it.

I didn't write this book because mothering little ones is easy for me. I wrote it because it isn't. I know that this is a hard job, because I am right here in the middle of it. I know you need encouragement every day, because I do too.

CHAPTER TWO

In the Rock Tumbler

I remember a time when I used to be much godlier. It was sometime in junior high and my room was clean. It must have been beautiful weather outside because the lighting was very nice in my room where I was reading my Bible every day and feeling really good. It was quite clear to me that my sanctification was progressing very well. As the feeling wore off, I remember looking back to that time as a high point. That was really living the Christian life.

The truth is my Christian life then was like a rock being refined by a slow river in a quiet place. It wasn't as though I wasn't growing spiritually, but my word! So easily! And so little!

But God took me out of that life and threw me into the rock tumbler. Here, it is not so easy to feel godly, because we spend our days crashing into each other and actually getting our problems addressed. Here there is very little time for quiet reflection. I do a lot of on-the-job failure and correction. Repenting and forgiving. Laughing. Lots and lots of laughing. Because if there is anything that life in the rock tumbler will teach you, it is that there is no room to take yourself seriously. Like trying to strike "cool" poses on a rug that someone is continually pulling out from under you, self-seriousness in mothering is totally pointless and probably painful!

The opportunities for growth and refinement abound here—but you have to be willing. You have to open your heart to the tumble. As you deal with your children, deal with yourself always and first. This is what it looks like and feels like to walk with God, as a mother.

God treats us with great kindness as we fail daily. He takes the long view of our sin—knowing that every time we fail and repent, we grow in our walk with Him. It is easy for us to accept this, because our sins are, well, ours.

But our children sin against us, annoy us, and mess up our stuff. We want to hold it against them, complain about them (if only to ourselves), and feel put upon by their sin. We have a much harder time accepting that every failure from them is a wonderful opportunity for repentance and growth and not an opportunity for us to exact penance.

It is no abstract thing—the state of your heart is the state of your home. You cannot harbor resentment secretly toward your children and expect their hearts to be submissive and tender. You cannot be greedy with your time and expect them to share their toys. And perhaps most importantly, you cannot resist your opportunities to be corrected by God and expect them to receive correction from you.

God has given us the job of teaching His law and demonstrating His grace. We are to be guides to our children as they learn to walk with God.

Sin is just a fact of life. It is the way we deal with it that changes ours.

CHAPTER THREE

Picky Chickens

Several years ago I was driving through Pennsylvania with some friends, and we stopped near the most gorgeous old farmhouse. Inside its large and fabulous yard there were a bunch of hilarious chickens running around. They must have been a variety of heirloom breeds—the colors and hairdos and feather leg warmers were just a little too outrageous for normal chickens, if you know what I mean! Anyway, we walked over to see them and they ran to us (presumably thinking we would offer them more than praise). But as soon as they got close, they were no longer the cute stuff. All of them had bald and bleeding spots where they had been picking one another's feathers out, the nasty little things.

These chickens came to my mind suddenly one day while I was trying to explain to my little girls why they may not fuss and bicker at each other, and it has since become its own offense in our home—being "picky chickens." My girls are of such an age that they get a big kick out of apologizing and returning feathers to each other. They actually have to say something like, "I love you because you are a sweet sister. I'm sorry I was picking at your feathers—here you go," and they exchange and return feathers and compliments. It has been our most successful picture of infighting, and a great tool for them to see themselves in their actions. I mean, honestly, who really likes the idea of being a mean chicken with open sores?

One of the great things about having children is that you constantly convict yourself by teaching them. If you are addressing their problems honestly, and if you double-check yourself, you will almost always find a little something to think about. Have you ever been frustrated by something your kids did? For me it is usually something I was not expecting—when the disobedience falls suddenly outside the normal range. Like filling up the bathroom sink with toothpaste and soap and shampoo. The need to correct is real, but so is the desire to pick a feather out while you are at it. Do you really want to be the fastest, biggest, pickiest, meanest chicken in the barnyard?

So think about your language with your children. When they disobey, do you talk about your own hurt? Are you pointing to all the work that you have to do now that they screwed up? Do you want to elaborate at all on how bad, bad, bad that particular thing was? Do you want to see them feel bad, or see them with a clear conscience so you can have a little snuggle tickle-fest?

I think we can all picture the kind of mother who sets a beautiful dinner on the table and then brings down all the people gathered around it with her nasty comments. Now try thinking of discipline as a different kind of nourishment—a sweet means of grace to your children. Bring that to the table with a smile and a wink—a means of building up little people, not a means of bringing them down. Make a point of telling them all about how you love them—with a lot of good solid points. Leave that table refreshed in your love for one another, and happy.

Of course life is real and life is earnest, and sometimes you just don't have time for a big chat over discipline because you are pretty sure you can hear someone playing with the microwave. But it doesn't take long to fluff feathers—you can do it on the go. One of the favorite techniques in our house is to periodically startle the kids by yelling, "Uh-oh!" and when they all look at you with concern you yell, "I love you!" It is funny every single time, and the kids know you wouldn't act that stupid if you didn't love them.

CHAPTER FOUR

Fruit of the Spirit Speed Quiz

Each day we get a sheet of paper with math problems on them. Except instead of basic addition and subtraction problems, they are little tests for our patience, for our peace, for our kindness. It is a regular fruit of the spirit speed quiz. They are easy, basic, Christian living challenges brought to us daily by our children, and the allotted time is our waking hours. Sometimes sporadically through the night.

We struggle our way through, and our score is not so good. So the next day, we will be given another test. As we get the hang of some problems, they disappear off the test and new, harder ones replace them. Eventually, the situation, which would have made us lose the bubble when we started the class, doesn't even cause us to hesitate. Easy peasy. Great! Time to move on!

My point here has to do with our attitudes, not only toward our own struggles, but toward the struggles that our children face. They are doing the same thing in their Christian lives.

It is very easy for us to forget about the progress they make and to ignore the problems that they no longer wrestle with. If you have been faithfully disciplining your children, I guarantee you that there are many, many problems that they no longer struggle with. Remember the era when they couldn't resist coloring on the walls? Or the times when so-and-so used to refuse to say "Amen"? Or back when going to bed was such a struggle?

As a parent it is very easy to demean their progress by demeaning the struggle. Instead of praising them and pointing to their progress to encourage them, we ignore it. We might even try to make them feel like they never make any progress. Like all these swats we give them are something they are failing to turn a profit on—"What's wrong with you? Why are you *still* doing this?" Sometimes this is because the struggle just seemed so dumb in the first place. Why our children have ever felt like it is a good idea to quickly unbuckle and dive over the back seat into the back hatch is beyond me. So when they quit doing it, we don't recognize they've gained the victory over a very real struggle with temptation. Oftentimes we don't even notice that they aren't doing it, because something else has replaced it, and we are now too busy nagging them about facing forward in the car.

Try to notice these little mile markers on the path of sanctification. If the sins have changed, it can be a sign of growth. It is not as though our children are going to emerge from their current problems into perfect holiness if only we give them enough swats. They are going to emerge from one set of problems into the next, and that is good. That is the way of the Christian walk. Treat sins that your children struggle with like basic math. Practice, practice, and you'll get it!

Another important aspect of this is that new problems come with age, whether or not we are ready for it. As parents, we are responsible to cover a certain amount of material, in a certain amount of time. If we get tired, distracted, or discouraged and stop teaching them, then they will very soon be in over their heads. Spiritual trigonometry is eventually coming for your children. It will really, really help them if they don't even need to think about basic multiplication by then! If your son in his high chair is struggling with anger about his vegetables, you should be seeing a high school boy acting out after a lost basketball game. Give him the tools now that he will need then.

If you have more than one child, it is especially easy to forget about their progress, because no sooner does one outgrow something than the next takes it up—like the Olympic torch. In fact, toothbrushes and the many evil deeds they incite has been a constant problem at our house for at least five years, but it has not been the same children wrestling with that temptation for all five years. In fact, it was only this afternoon that I had to grab a wet wipe on my way out the door to remove some toothpaste from the side of my shoe. I don't even know who did it (but I could narrow the field of suspects, because one of our children has finished their leg of the toothpaste race and one is not yet running).

So while this should remind us to encourage our children, it should also encourage us. The discipline does work. We *are* making progress with our children. And if you have been faithfully repenting of your own failures and looking for chances to grow, you are making progress too. You might feel just as tired, but you are now running ten miles instead of two blocks. Take a moment to remember what used to annoy you when you were single—are you done howling with laughter yet? Do you see how totally unchallenging that looks now?

Especially for those of us who have a bunch of little ones and feel like we have been talking about not fussing on endless repeat since some time in 2003, it is good to stop and look back and see that the journey really is taking us somewhere. So don't give up! Don't think that the endless trips off to the bathroom for correction with a toddler or two are just a waste of time and energy—it is a gift that you are giving to your children. They will need these life skills! You are repeating these things for them just like a teacher circling missed math problems with a red pen. They will get it eventually, they just need lots and lots of repetition.

It is this repetition that discourages parents of little ones. You can feel like the only thing you do all day every day is tell the kids to stop. Stop fussing, stop touching, stop fighting, stop asking, stop being awake, and anything else you can think of that you would like for them to stop. Are you having to circle almost every problem on every student's test every day? Are you starting to write the grade on the top of the page a little bigger and with a stern face? Are you going to try to drum up some of those Mr. Poison stickers to start putting on papers?

When this happens, a summary for the day might be something like this: "Child number one was a huge pill all day. Child number two was crying and fussing and fighting with child number one. Children three and four were just as bad, but I don't know what they were doing, but everyone was terrible, terrible, terrible. Nothing was good all day. Twelve percent for everyone. *An F minus for the whole class.* We failed, flunked, bombed out, and were ugly, ugly, ugly today. The only thing left for us is to cry ourselves to sleep, because nothing can fix the kind of mess we're in."

Imagine you give a report like this to your husband at the end of the day while collapsed on the couch making tired faces. Then imagine that he asks in his unhelpful way if you were spanking for it. (Don't pretend you haven't had a conversation like this some time—I know all about it!) Usually the answer would be not really, or very little. Because when you come right down to it, you know exactly who needs to be spanked, and it is you. Because if you are the teacher and none of the students are succeeding, you need to be doing a better job. You need to think of new ways to explain the lessons. Change up the terminology a bit. Give some illustrations.

Here is an example: a while ago our older girls were slipping into being less than subtle about their preferences at the dinner table. We were having lots of bossy, rude, superior comments about the food, the seating arrangement, whatever. For many reasons they could not see our point. "But I do think it looks gross!" While we kept saying "Don't be rude," they would respond with "Okay, but I don't want to sit next to him." It just wasn't getting through.

So we tried telling them a story about a lady who lived in a beautiful palace. We would tell about her garden, her clothes, her jewelry, her smile, her laughing. And then we would tell about someone coming to get her for dinner and how she came to the table where the dinner was waiting for her and all of her friends were there and how she said (in a very loud, ugly voice), "Oh yuck! I hate this! And I don't want to sit next to you!"

Suddenly they understood. In the context of the story, they could hear the missed note at the end.

Setting behaviors into stories is a great way to communicate with your little people. Got a boy hitting a sister? Tell him about a brave knight who went out to fight the dragon but started hitting the princess instead. Give the children a chance to get outside themselves and see their behavior as it plays out in a story. It often turns out that they know exactly the right thing to do.

CHAPTER FIVE

Spirited Riders

I have a little flock of daughters. With four of them five years old and under, it should come as no surprise to you that we deal with a walloping share of emotions at our house. Titus is so simple (of course, he is also still two years old)—just right up the middle and easy. He either disobeys, or he doesn't. Sometimes, when he feels really complicated and deep, he fusses. I am sure he will grow into more difficult problems (competition for one), but right now there are no subtexts with this kid. He wants milk—that is why he is fussing and saying, "I want milk!" Not so complex—even a beginner parent can figure out a technique to deal with this. But girls are different, and sometimes that difference can leave a person completely bewildered. When it comes to little girls and their emotions, *A* does not necessarily cause *B*. But when *B* is what needs to be disciplined, it can feel frustrating to have no clues as to what member of the alphabet actually caused it. Are you with me here?

One of our sweet little girls has a hilarious tendency that we refer to as her "drunk driving." If she is tired, she becomes reckless and disobedient. Her eyes get a little glassy, she gets super rowdy, and you might find her unloading the freezer or coloring her sheets with a marker or some such clearly outlawed activity. Once, when she was in the midst of one of these times, I caught her on the kitchen counter getting into something. Surprise was my first response—"What are you *doing?*" Her immediate response was to throw her hands up over her eyes in shame. It was at that moment I realized that she didn't know what was causing it either! She was just as surprised as I was to find herself being so delinquent. It wasn't any kind of deep malice that got her into those cupboards looking for chocolate chips— it was just a simple lack of control.

I was so thankful for that little glimpse into what was causing what with this little person, and it has really shaped the way we deal with all kinds of behavioral issues. Sometimes parents can discipline behaviors over and over and over like we are playing whack-a-mole. There is a sin! Get it! This can get very frustrating when it doesn't seem to be helping anything. We think we are being so diligent! But the real problem is that the child doesn't know what to do with it.

Say it is someone else's birthday. Say your child wants a present too. Say they start fussing about it. Imagine that then you say, "Don't do that. That is bad. Don't be a fusser. Deal with it." How did that help anyone? The child is taught that if the feeling comes over them, they have already failed. That is bad! But what am I supposed to do with it? It doesn't just go away by itself. Little girls need help sorting out their emotions—not so they can wallow in them, but so they can learn to control them.

We tell our girls that their feelings are like horses—beautiful, spirited horses. But they are the riders. We tell them that God gave them this horse when they were born, and they will ride it their whole life. God also set us on a path on the top of a mountain together and told us to follow it. We can see for a long way—there are beautiful flowers, lakes, trees, and rainbows. (We are little girls after all!) This is how we "walk in the light as He is in the light, and have fellowship with one another" (1 Jn. 1:7).

When our emotions act up, it is like the horse trying to jump the fence and run down into a yucky place full of spiders to get lost in the dark. A good rider knows what to do when the horse tries to bolt—you pull on the reins! Turn the horse's head! Get back on the path! We also tell our girls that God told us if we see one of them with her horse down in a mud puddle spitting at people who walk by, it is our job to haul them up, willing or unwilling, back to the path. The ways that this has helped me as a mother are pretty obvious, but I will share them anyway if you will bear with me.

First of all, the horses are not the problem. There is nothing wrong with the emotions. If we have a little rider who is woefully unprepared to control her horse, well then, we had better start with some pretty serious riding lessons. Talk to your daughters about how they might feel, and what you want to see when they do. Give them some practical handholds; be a coach. Anticipate moments that might be hard, when the horse might bolt, and help them learn to anticipate it too. Take a little break to say, "Hey sweetie, we are going in this store, but we aren't going to buy any toys today. If you start feeling like you want to fuss about it, what are we going to do?" Make a plan. Use code words. Wink. Encourage. Give lots of praise when you see her overcoming little emotional temptations. Be right there with her as she learns to recognize what is happening. Little girls can be scared out of their minds when their emotions charge off with them. They need the security of parents pulling them back.

The goal is not to cripple the horse, but equip the rider. A well-controlled passionate personality is a powerful thing. That is what dangerous women are made of. But a passionate personality that is unbridled can cause a world of damage. If you see a lot of passion in your little girls, don't be discouraged. It is just wonderful raw material. Our house is pretty near full to overflowing with this kind of raw material! But don't treat it lightly either—runaway horses can be a very real threat to your little girls.

CHAPTER SIX

Heavy Branches

When I was in junior high and early high school, we lived in an old farmhouse that had grown into the middle of town. In the side yard, right outside my window, were two old apple trees. And year after year they made apples. I clearly remember lying in bed at night and hearing the apples falling off the tree—not occasionally, but continually. They were just thumping on the ground all through the night. And these trees had been throwing apples on the ground every August for probably ninety years or so. It is something I love about fruit-bearing trees and bushes—that God told them to make something, and they do it enthusiastically. They don't care about what happens to the fruit. They do not measure their efforts or fuss when no one appreciates it.

My mind has been wandering around, thinking about fruit a lot lately—a friend had me over to pick blackberries off of her insanely productive blackberry patch, and then we went to an orchard to press cider. These little fruit-oriented events got me thinking about the nature of fruitfulness. Just what does being fruitful look like?

If you are like me, probably one of the first things you think of is Psalm 128: "Your wife will be like a fruitful vine within your house; your children will be like olive shoots around your table."

But the funny thing is that in this verse, the fruitful vine is not bearing children, she is bearing fruit. The children were all off her vine long ago and are responsible for their own fruit-bearing. She is just a heavy laden vine. My mom has always taught that fruitfulness is not equal to bearing children, and here is another example of that. The mere fact of having had children does not mean you are a fruitful person. That would be like the apple trees calling it off after their first year of bearing fruit.

But true fruitfulness requires constant, year-round attention. It requires taking risks. It might mean making a truckload of apples to throw in a ditch out in the country somewhere. It is funny to think about, but God does not tell us to necessarily be strategic with our fruit. We do not need to know what will happen to the fruit. Will someone check on it every day? Harvest the best to make a pie? Or will there be a junior high kid sweating around among the yellow jackets trying to pick it all up—wishing that we were not quite so bountiful? What happens to all our fruit is not our problem. That doesn't mean that we are not to care about the fruit. While it is on our branches, it is our life work. It is an offering to God, and we ought to care intensely about the quality of our fruit. But the branches are our responsibility; the ground is not.

But what does this apply to in real life? Well, think about yourself and about the things you do. Look at it like fruit. Are you holding yourself back on things, afraid that the end result will not be worthy of your labor? Are you afraid to fail? Is there some domestic activity that you would love to know how to do, but don't want to try in case it doesn't turn out? Are you afraid to try new recipes? Are you afraid to put energy or money into something that might turn into nothing? Do you think fondly of some day when you might bear fruit, but resist getting right down to business this year? Do you evaluate the necessity of everything, passing it by if it doesn't add up to be practical? Are you limiting the branches upon which you are willing to bear fruit?

I think that in some ways we have let our cultural admiration for efficiency get into places that it doesn't belong. Speaking for myself, sometimes I am working away on something and just cannot shake the question "Why am I doing this? Is this a ridiculous use of my time? Should I be doing something that matters, rather than (say) knitting a costumed mouse?" But it is very freeing to laugh at yourself—laugh when you know that apple you were working on may very well fall to the ground, and who cares? But the chances are good that the more fruit you make the more fruit gets used. The more you throw yourself into heavy branches, the more inviting the fruit, and the more inviting the fruit, the more people it is likely to feed.

Some of those apples will fall to the ground and rot. But God uses rotten apples—to fertilize the ground, to start more apple trees after little animals plant them, and just to make the air smell sticky sweet. You cannot know the depth of His plan for your fruit. So throw it out there on the ground when you have no plan for its future. Waste it. Waste homemade pasta (and the mess it makes) on your family. Don't save cloth napkins for company only—sew a dress your daughter doesn't really need. Be bountiful with your fruit and free with it. The only thing that you can know for certain is that God will use it.

CHAPTER SEVEN

Thanksters & Cranksters

As any parent of little children knows, being in the car can be quite the challenge. There are often little disagreements in the back seat that are somewhat obtuse in origin. Someone may have made an ugly face at someone else, which caused that person to make an ugly noise, which caused another to burst into tears, and when you pull over and turn around, everyone is pointing at someone else.

Even if there is no infighting, being in the car seems to commence open season on complaining. Our children develop a desperate thirst almost upon entering the vehicle. It is just easy to find a lot to complain about, sitting there in the back seat elbowing each other.

We have developed a little system for talking about this in our family that is called "Thanksters or Cranksters." The basic gist of it is quite easy. Thanksters look for things they *do* have; Cranksters look for things they *don't* have. Luckily for us, our last name allows for a third category of "Janksters," but that is not essential to the plan. Thankfulness is a great antidote to fussing— but it is hard to get your kids to feel thankful right in the middle of a fuss, right?

Sometimes we use the trick of saying, "I know, it is so sad for you that you don't have any brothers or sisters!" or "Too bad you don't have any legs so you can't run." or "I am so sorry that you don't even have a home." This always makes the kids laugh, but it teaches a good lesson too. There are abundant things to be thankful for that are not on our radar at the current moment. So you have a headache. So the kids are fussing. Well, are you looking at what you don't have (energy and quiet) or what you do have (a head and kids)?

I know this seems painfully obvious, but when our children are fussing, the antidote for them is gratitude. But how are we showing them that when we start getting huffy and snippy? Are you modeling thankfulness by being thankful for your fussy children as you are all overstimulated in a car with foggy windows? You might be thinking to yourself that you would be happy if only you could get a coffee and the kids would stop. Well, they are back in the back seat thinking that they would stop fussing if only the parents would let them have a milkshake and go to Pizza Hut. There you are the both (or all) of you doing the same thing.

So make sure that before you start rebuking them, your own heart is in order. Thank God for the headache.

Thank Him for these prime opportunities to teach. Thank Him for the scuffle that your children are currently having over who unbuckled whom and why. And then, after your own heart has been sorted out, move on to theirs.

So do a little test run with your kids. Ask them things like, "What would a Crankster do right now?" Our kids get a kick out of trying to drum up the most random things to complain about to make each other laugh. It really helps them to see a fussy attitude as petty and foolish. Then we talk about what a Thankster would see. Look out your window at things that you ought to be thankful for. Do you see rain? What would we do without water? Do you see sunshine? And birds to sing? Can you use your eyes? Do you have a nose? Is there a baby we love in the car? Can you tell that autumn is coming? And the point of all these questions . . . aren't you blessed?

CHAPTER EIGHT

Watch Your Language

Children are linguistic sponges. If you say something, so will they. Obviously coarse or off-color language is something that Christian parents ought to avoid because it is something that Christians ought to avoid. But what about words like *stupid, idiot, dummy, shut up,* and all the rest? At some point in your parenting career you will hear one of your kids pop off with one of these. It is certainly not a great idea for them to be freelancing with words like this, so you tell them they may not say it. Then, usually a little later in the day, you will find yourself saying, "I feel so stupid!" or the neighbor lady is saying, "Oh my word! Shut up! That is so funny!" and you realize that your children are watching with curiosity and already forming questions about your double standard. At the same time, you know it would be a strange legalism that would ban these from your house altogether.

My husband dealt with this problem by talking to the kids about the nature of words. Words are tools, and some of them are like the big kitchen knives—you have to be big enough to use them. If little kids start saying "stupid" or "idiot," it is like they are playing with the knives. They are not big enough to control what they cut. They will start hurting each other and cutting their own fingers. So, these words are just like the knives— they are a "no touch." But they may watch and listen now so that they can learn how to use them. Of course, if you are using these words to cut down your husband or friends, then you will need to stop doing that—they can be just as destructive to a grown person.

Another way in which we can do damage to ourselves is through the use of totally innocent words that we use to allow ourselves something. I remember thinking sometimes when the twins were little that I had better stop being *overwhelmed*.

This was normal now. For a few months there in the middle of the wet, gray, rainy part of winter, I had two nursing infants and two toddlers— three out of four in diapers. It was very physically, as well as emotionally, intense. I can remember around this time taking the garbage out and just standing outside the door taking some deep breaths, getting ready to go back in. (When taking the garbage out becomes a "destination," you know you are really in the trenches!) It was somewhere around this time that I realized I had better strike the word *overwhelmed* from my vocabulary.

God gave me this to do. I may not be overwhelmed about it. I can try as hard as I can, and maybe fail sometimes. I can try as hard as I can and fall asleep at the dinner table. I can try as hard as I can and be completely burned out at the end of the day. But I may not be overwhelmed. Actually, I may be overwhelmed, but I may not say that I am overwhelmed! The words have a real power over us. If you say it, you allow it for yourself. You give yourself that little bit of room to say, "But I can't!"

When God gives us children, it is work that He is giving us. Work that comes with huge attendant blessings and bonuses, but work nonetheless. So imagine yourself delegating a task to someone (your children come to mind). Imagine you are asking them to clean up a room. You can see the work that you are giving them. You know that they need to pick up the dress-ups, the plastic food, and the books. You also know that what you are asking is well within their abilities. Now imagine one child looks at it, takes a deep breath, and dives in. But the other picks up one piece of food and then lies down to cry a bit about all the rest of them. You know as a parent that lying down and whimpering about the tasks does not get them done. It makes them harder, slower, and more difficult in every way. The child who is really working faithfully will see progress, will see that the task is doable. The child who is feeling sorry for himself will never get past that emotional low without some disciplinary intervention.

Do you see yourself in that? When you get up in the morning and the house is a mess, and the kids are being a little eggy, and you didn't get to the grocery store, do you like to drape yourself across the work that God gave you and whimper? Or do you just dive in? Do you take a few steps and then go limp? Do you like to dwell on the discouragement? Do you spend time not working but tallying the work that you think is too much for you?

After having the twins, I had to deal with this because it was easy to get overwhelmed. I can remember telling my husband that I was going to try not to say that anymore, not even to myself. It was time for me to adjust to the work load that God had given me. But deciding to be the kid who would dive in and not the kid who would stand around anticipating the work and getting overwhelmed has some real consequences. You have to know that you are giving up those moments that you were allowing yourself. Deciding not to say it is different than never actually being in over your head. But God loves a cheerful worker. I am still frequently in over my head. Actually, most of the time! But deciding to not wallow in that fact has removed one of the biggest obstacles to my work—my own calculations of how hard the job is.

If you decide to do this (and I strongly recommend you do), you will need to tell someone. Tell the people you are most likely to complain to—your husband, your mother, your sister, your friend. Tell them you are not going to say "____" anymore. Whatever terminology you use to allow yourself a little self-pity. It is pretty funny how much this feels like jumping off the high dive, and it can make you realize how much you were using that little excuse. I am sure that I still say "overwhelmed" from time to time, but it is no longer that little crutch for droopiness that it once was to me.

Instead of spending time telling yourself stories in which you are given too much to do, come up with some simple coping tactics. In that same early and intense phase with the twins, I developed the twenty-minute rule. If things started seeming really out of control, I would look at the clock and note the time. Then I would tell myself that in twenty minutes this would be over.

If I just kept my head down and did the work, twenty minutes was all I needed. And actually, it was true. Twenty minutes is enough time (if you are moving quickly and not moping) to change three diapers and one complete outfit, spank one disobeyer, tuck two people into naps, and sit down to nurse the other two. The storm would have passed in twenty minutes if I was cheerfully getting things done. But that moment when you first discovered the blowout, and then the two-year-old hit the one-year-old (who is now having a naptime meltdown with a dirty diaper), and both of the babies were mad because we were in the car when they decided it was lunchtime, and now, thirty minutes later, you still haven't nursed them, but first you've got to change the whole outfit and maybe can't find the clothes . . . well, that moment. What was it? A moment. It passes. But when it passes, you will be very glad if all you did was work right through it. No self-pity, no tears, no getting worked into a dither. Look at the clock, look at the work you need to do, and bear down. That super intensity will almost always be over in twenty minutes!

CHAPTER NINE

To the Fifth Power

Something we discovered when we had the twins is the concept of the "bulk effect." Our OB told us in advance that having the twins was not going to make us twice as busy (we had two at the time), but rather exponentially busier, and he was right. Every time you add a child to your family, you are not just increasing the total sum—you are exponentially increasing.

The thing that we had to realize was that the twins were not super fussy babies—there was just twice as much baby fussing. Since we cheated and skipped right to four children, I don't really know about the three-kid scene, but I am pretty sure that three is the tipping point. Up until three, it is easy to see your kids as individuals and their actions as exclusively their own. After three, they all start running together a bit.

Let's say that you are trying to get ready for church, and one child is disobedient (something petty, like not putting on their shoes when you told them to). They wandered off and got distracted and loitered in the living room for a minute. In that minute the baby starts crying, you see the clock and realize that you are going to be late, you can't find the wet wipes or the baby's shoe, which you know you put on the table last night. The baby is still screaming, so you are trying to rock the car seat with your foot while doing the hair of your middle child who will not stop bouncing. You are shouting out to your husband to see if he knows what happened to the baby shoe, probably punctuated with "Sit still. Stop. Don't wiggle." As it turns out, your husband is out looking for someone's lost shoe in the car where they are prone to remove them, so you get no response. You begin to have evil thoughts about shoes. You start feeling the pressure, if you know what I mean. The tension is mounting. You may very well be feeling hot and sweaty while your coffee is getting cold on the counter, untouched. At this moment, the child who didn't put his shoes on comes wandering back, refreshed with a nice spell of magna-doodling. What do you think happens?

You take that shred of guilt and then harness onto it the stress of the whole situation. You make your child into a scapegoat, a way for you to release all of your tension and stress onto someone who you feel deserved it. He did, after all, disobey. Your massive overreaction was just, because disobeying is wrong. So this neat little trick is happening in your head—the consequences for his sin go way up, and the consequences for yours go way down. It is simply a classic shifting of the blame. The situation is crazy, but you are the person responsible to get the grace to deal with it.

Oftentimes you won't even discipline the sin that did occur, because you are wanting to leave this situation with the feeling that you were full of grace toward that child who maliciously magna-doodled. Next time, you say, you will get spankings. This time, you will just have to bear the weight of my discontent, my anger, and my lack of self-control. I will vent on you instead of dealing with myself. So let that be a lesson to you about quick obeying. Do it just like I do—that is, fail completely if you get distracted.

If you took the actions of each individual child, nothing big happened. One kid took her shoes off last night in the car. One kid keeps bouncing when you are trying to fix her hair, one kid had a dirty diaper, and one kid magna-doodled instead of putting on shoes, and the baby just wants some attention. And of course the disobeying is wrong. The combined effect is certainly ripe, especially when you add in the things that Mom and Dad were responsible for. The time. The lost clothing that could have been found last night. Not noticing the distracted disobedience right away. Not getting up early enough to drink your coffee. Not getting grace to deal with it as soon as it started heating up.

The situation is not a sin. It is merely the combined effect of a lot of people. And just because you can pin down one sin in the batch does not mean that child is responsible for the situation. Your children are not a situation. They are individuals. Disciplining an individual for a collective situation is a great way to alienate your children. It is not only unjust and unkind, but it is untrue to the gospel. Christ takes our sins; He does not load us down with someone else's. He sees what we have done and takes it from us and bears it with Him to the cross. What you just did was toss your burden of guilt onto a child to have her carry it. Well, what is she supposed to do with it, other than be beaten down by it?

So the "bulk effect" is what happens when there are a lot of children, and it will happen from time to time. Individually, there is nothing to worry about. As a group, it feels as though we are careening toward destruction. If you have a bunch of little kids (or even a few), you will need to not only be aware of this fact of life, but build up your immunity to it. You will need to see it happening and get the grace for it in advance. You will need to develop some skills for coping with it that do not involve blaming your children.

CHAPTER TEN

Know Your Sheep

Another way that we try to counteract the bulk effect and treat our children as individuals is simply by realizing that it is not their fault that there are so many of them. The fact that there are five of them is our problem, not theirs. In situations where the number of children actually is a problem, it is our responsibility to deal with it.

Just because we have a bunch of children does not mean that they ought to be living in a military dictatorship. Dry erase boards and chore charts are all well and good, but they do not change the fact that what you have on your hands is children, not an organizational problem. When Scripture says to bring them up in the nurture and admonition of the Lord, it is not talking about finding the most effective way to organize them. This is a very easy trap to fall in, because the more children you have the more difficult it is to keep them clean and clothed and fed. Just the basics of life are a full-time job.

It is also easy for parents to fall into this sort of lifestyle because cleaning and sorting makes you look and maybe even feel like you have your act together, even if you seriously don't. What you are doing is finding a way to contain your children, control them, and keep their sin from making you look bad. But you are not actually dealing with anything. The fact that your children have learned to go with the household flow and do their chores does not in any way offset the fact that they spend all their available free time sulking in their room. Christian childrearing is a pastoral pursuit, not an organizational challenge.

The more children you have, the more you need to be pastorally minded. Look to each of their souls and their needs. If you are focused on upkeep of the house and the schedule, as long as your child is not interrupting that, you don't worry about it. If you are being a parent who is pastorally minded, you will stop whatever it is that you are doing to go see how your daughter is up in her bedroom. Has she been quiet lately? Was that a faint door-slam you heard in the distance? Find out about that. Did one of your kids seem a touch off as they went outside to sit in a tree? Don't let that go. Be a pastor to your children. Study them. Seek them out. Sacrifice the thing you were doing to work through minor emotional issues.

A lot of children from big families discover very early on that their parents simply do not have time for their problems. So they find ways to take care of themselves, usually through adapting to loneliness.

This is why you may have known families who seemed to have it all together. Everyone to his own military bunk. Dinner from the crockpot at 6:00 p.m. on the dot. Family worship in the living room. Children quietly doing the dishes afterwards. Then, as the children hit their teen years, you start to see that alongside all that organization was some serious neglect and hurt. It is possible to organize your children right out of the church. So while your children are little, cultivate an attitude of sacrifice. Sacrifice your peace for their fun, your clean kitchen floor for their help cracking eggs, your quiet moment for their long retelling of a dream that a friend of theirs allegedly had. Prioritize your children far and away above the other work you need to get done. They are the only part of your work that really matters.

My children love to help in the kitchen. Since my oldest is five, she is only now starting to really be a help. Actually, I take that back because my four-year-old just showed some extreme gingersnap-shaping skills. However, the rest of them just love to be involved. It turns out that one child in a Baby Bjorn and four more in the kitchen on chairs trying to help knead the bread can be a little overstimulating. But the thing that I have had to learn is that it is my job to figure out how to make this work. If I only had one child, these sorts of excited inquiries into "Whatcha doin'?" followed by the "Can I help you, Mama?" would be received with an enthusiastic and loving welcome.

But when there is a whole chorus of voices and a whole army of chairs moving into the kitchen, bringing out the enthusiastic welcome is a lot harder. I have to adapt. It is not their problem. Individually they are being precious and curious and excited. As their mother, I am responsible to see them individually, even when they are presenting themselves to me *en masse*.

I can clearly remember one night when I was big pregnant with Blaire and realized too late that we were out of tortillas. I figured I would just make some quickly. When I started this project I was alone in the kitchen. About a minute and a half into it I had been discovered. Four chairs into the kitchen, four children anxiously awaiting a chance to help. I remember Titus actually bumping into the back of my legs with his chair and very politely saying, "Excuse me, Mama! 'Scuse me!" Then came the real action: Titus wildly dusting flour on the tortilla I was rolling, someone cracking into the drawer and passing out rolling pins. Everyone rolling, and dusting, and rolling, and wadding the dough back up and having a grand old time too. I looked out of the haze of flour and elbows feeling very ready to blow the whistle, and I saw my husband smiling at me and laughing. He nodded at me and said, "It's okay." I knew what he meant. Fat souls are better than clean floors. They were so delighted to be in the thick of it—dinner was late, I could have slept standing up, and we were doing exactly the right thing—throwing flour around the kitchen. And it *was* okay. I don't even remember cleaning it up (quite likely because I was asleep on the couch while Luke did it all!). The details of how far the flour was spread escape me now, but I remember the fun they had. Most of the time the children do not know that what they are doing is overwhelming. This is because they do not forget that they are individuals.

Now I am not saying that there are not times when I just say, "Sorry kids, not a good time for helpers." Once Daphne came in while I was cooking and asked to help. I told her I didn't really have a good job for her right then. After a pause she said, "Well . . . do you have a bad one?" There are plenty of these moments. It is just that very often it is a fine time for helpers—even a good time for them, if I am willing to get the grace for it.

CHAPTER ELEVEN

Fire Alarms

I don't know about how the rest of you are, but personally I like a clean and orderly house. This is by no means saying that that is what I have, but it is what I like. I work for it, daily sweeping what must be pounds of debris off of my floors, struggling with an unearthly amount of unmatched socks, and surveying under beds for ancient sippy cup or bottle carnage. Sometimes we go for almost a whole week with a pretty clean house! But occasionally something happens and everything collapses. Like the stomach virus or Christmas—remarkably similar effects on the house when you think about it! Or as happened in my case, you get laid up for a week, while the children press on with regular to abnormally high energy levels. There is a substantial part of me that gets wound up looking at a dirty house and another part that thinks it is justified to do so.

After all, it is okay to want a clean house, right? It is important for the children, right? It is foul and depraved to have crumbs sticking to your socks and not take action, right? These are all good instincts, right? Right. They are. We do in fact care about cleanliness. We also love clean clothes. Furthermore, everyone does in fact appreciate a clean bathroom. This is all very true.

Now stay with me for a moment as I leap into an uncharted metaphor. We have fire alarms, and we keep them around to awaken us if there is a fire in the middle of the night, and we need to run out of the house only grabbing our children. That is what my cleaning instincts are like—they are in place to keep the house from going up in dust-bunny flames. But here is the problem: sometimes it was not the house burning down so much as it was just a burnt piece of toast. And we all know from experience that fire alarms are not to be trusted for perspective in these situations. Neither are your instincts. There are times when the only thing to do is remove the batteries. Turn it off. Stop panicking about the long-term effects of yucky fridge shelves. Let it go for a minute. Open the door and wave a cookie sheet around or something!

CHAPTER TWELVE

Me Time

This is something that I am sure every mother has heard about. You just need a little time to yourself. A long bath, some time to do your nails, getting your hair done, or going shopping for the day. We all need a little time off every once in a while. My husband likes to send me out to go look at yarn or have coffee with some friends. And all these things are great, in so much as they leave you refreshed for the work you do.

Taking a little time for yourself is absolutely needed. I remember the first time that having the twins threatened my morning shower. They just needed me, and needed me, and needed me until it was getting pretty late, and I hadn't gotten out of my pajamas. Then suddenly I had an idea. I would just put them in their crib and take a shower. They could cry for a few minutes—they were fed, and clean, and they would be all right. I was not fed, or clean, and I would not be all right. So I popped them in their crib and said "I'll be back in a few minutes—have fun!" and off I went. As I recall I took a speed shower and then read my Bible for a few minutes.

All this to say, I am officially on the record in favor of "me time." It is necessary and fabulous. It isn't good for the kids to have a frazzled and unshowered mother, so by all means get that kind of thing done. Find a way. Turn on a cartoon if you must—it isn't the end of the world.

But there is a sense in which we must really guard ourselves. Motherhood is a demanding job. It is so demanding and intrusive, in fact, that it takes over your body. It uses your body, oftentimes rather roughly. This can start to bother us. You may have some weight to lose, and you might start to resent that. You might have permanently damaged something during a pregnancy. You may have big scars, stretch marks, and loose skin that bothers you. You might not have time to exercise the way you used to. All of these things can be seen as an offense against us—against our bodies.

There are really two separate points I would like to make here. First of all, our bodies are tools, not treasures. You should not spend your days trying to preserve your body in its eighteen-year-old form. Let it be used. By the time you die, you want to have a very dinged and dinted body. Motherhood uses your body in the way that God designed it to be used. Those are the right kind of damages.

There are of course ways to hurt your body that are outside of God's design for it and disobedient. But motherhood is what your stomach was made for—and any wear and tear that it shows is simply the sign of a well-used tool. We are not to treat our bodies like museum pieces. They were not given to us to preserve, they were given to us to use. So use it cheerfully, and maintain it cheerfully. When you are working hard to lose the baby weight (as you may need to), think of it as tool maintenance. You want to fix your body up in order to be able to use it some more. It might be used for more children, or it might be used to take care of the children you have. We should not be trying to fix it up to put it back on the shelf out of harm's way or to try to make ourselves look like nothing ever happened. Your body is a tool. Use it.

Also, your body is a tool—maintain it. Having sacrificed your body for your children is no excuse for schlepping around in sweatpants for the rest of their childhood. When you were eighteen, you might have been skinny without trying. In your thirties, after having had a pile of kids, the chances are good that you will need to try. And in case you care, this word is not coming from one of those miracle mothers who comes out of the hospital more svelte than she went in! My children, bless them, have left their mark!

Scars and stretch marks and muffin tops are all part of your kingdom work. One of the greatest testimonies Christian women can have in our world today is the testimony of joyfully giving your body to another. While so many women choose to not have children or abort the children that they were given, the testimony of women who know the cost and joyfully pay it is profound. So make sure that you aren't buying into the world's propaganda. While there are a great many rewards, the sacrifice is very real. The reason so many women don't want to do it is because it is very hard and has very real costs. But the answer to these obstacles is not to run away in fear as the world does, but to meet it with joy, and in faith.

My very kind and wise husband once left a note for me on Easter morning, two weeks after Daphne was born. He wrote, "To my wife, before she even goes near the closet on Easter morning," or something romantic like that. In it, he encouraged me to realize that there was no more fitting way to celebrate Easter (or any part of the Christian life) than in a body that has been undone on behalf of another.

So realize that your body is a testimony to the world of God's design. Carry the extra weight joyfully until you can lose it joyfully. Carry the scars joyfully as you carry the fruit of them. Do not resent the damages that your children left on your body. Just like a guitar mellows and sounds better with age and scratches, so your body can more fully praise God having been used for His purposes. So don't resent it, enjoy it.

Second, the world has a very muddled perception of "self." They think and tell us to think that we are all little separate entities who might need to go off somewhere to get to know "ourselves," or that a mother needs to get back to her corporate job to be herself again. Marriages break up because people don't know who they are anymore. They need to find themselves.

But the Christian view of self is very different, and you need to make sure that it is the one you have. We are like characters in a story. Our essential self is not back in the intro, waiting to be rediscovered. Who you are is where you are. When you are married, your essential self is married. As the story grows, so does your character. Your children change you into a different person. If you suddenly panic because it all happened so fast and now you don't recognize yourself, what you need is not time alone. What you need is your people. Look out—look at the people who made you what you are—your husband and your children. Study them. They are you. If you want to know yourself, concentrate on them.

Those women who try to find themselves by stripping away the "others" will find that they are a very broken little thing. This will lead them to resent the people who they think made them that way. She may say, "I used to be so energetic, but all these people take, take, take from me and now I have no time to just be me!" And the world gathers around and comforts her and says she needs some time to follow her dreams.

But the Christian woman needs to see, "I used to be so boring! Now my character has some depth, some people to love, some hardships to bear. Now I have some material to work with." A Christian woman's view is always forward and never back. Your identity is to be found and resting in other people.

Let me try this from another angle. As married Christian women, our identity is in our husbands. We are their helpmeets. Our calling is people-oriented. It follows then that you cannot know what your calling is until you know *who* your calling is. Until you are married, you are not tied to a specific person. Marriage reorients you entirely. Children do even more. Then it is your calling to help your husband by raising these little people. People, people everywhere and no time for yourself. But remember that this is your calling. It belongs to you. They belong to you.

If you want some quality "me time," make a date with your husband. Do something special with your children. These people are you. Your identity is supposed to be intertwined—that is the way God wrote the story, and it is the way He intends us to read it.

CHAPTER THIRTEEN

See Your Children

I love how babies are hard to decipher at first. You spend all that time in your pregnancy wondering, "Who is this little person?" and then she is born and you look at her and think, "Who is this little person?"

Throughout their childhood they continue to reveal themselves to you. Like a mystery seed you planted, they show more and more of the personality that God put in as they develop the tools to express it.

Come along with me for a little detour here. Let's say that your gifts and your talents and your personality have made you a tomato plant. Then let's say that you married a tomato plant. You settle down and plan to raise a nice crop of other tomato plants in your own little hothouse. Maybe you have one child—a nice little tomato. Then another. But as this child grows, you start to realize that it is not a tomato! This is starting to look more like a watermelon! What now? There is no sin in being a watermelon, but it can be a very hard life if you were born into the family of tomatoes.

Parents the whole world over fall into the temptation of wanting their children to share their loves, and grow up to be just like them. Sometimes, by nature, the children do. Everything is so easy! No one has to change.

Let's say that you and your husband are real readers who think there's nothing more fun than a used bookstore or a quiet afternoon at home. Maybe your first child takes on the exact same loves. But somehow, because God has a sense of humor and loves to make us grow, He bestowed, to your care, a natural-born party planner. In this situation, who is responsible to grow? Does your child need to sacrifice his or her abilities and desires on the little altar of Mom-likes-a-quiet-house? Or does Mom need to lay it out for her child and get the grace to not only accommodate, but appreciate and love that personality? It is the parents' responsibility to help the children refine their gifts. If their gifts are not the same as yours, the first step is to own them as though they are. You are no longer just a quiet family. You are a family that loves to have parties and also quiet evenings. You have officially expanded your skill set. Oftentimes, our children's gifts will take us places that we never intended, but needed, to go.

I have heard more than one mother try to head off growth like this at the pass. Announcing to whoever wants to listen that they don't do hair. That they hate to shop. That this girly thing is way out of their league.

Essentially what they are saying is that they are afraid of the new territory that God set before them. If this sounds familiar to you, you are going to need to get over it. Oftentimes the reason a mother is in such an insecure place about it is because her own mother didn't come alongside her. You'll want to break that pattern! So get busy. You can ask other people to help, but you need to get in and get involved. Figure it out. Own it, and don't complain about it.

As we find out about our children, we will begin to see their virtues as well as their vices. Parents need to keep in mind that their children are not simple. Personalities manifest in things that are good and bad. But the bad things very often are manifestations of good things, and the good things are manifestations of bad things. This is simply an elaborate way of saying that your virtues are your vices are your virtues.

It is easy enough to interpret the ways in which your children differ from you as vices (because there are two sides of everything) and the things that they share with you as virtues. But trying to whittle a watermelon down to a tomato will impair its growth and still not make a tomato. You will end up hurting your children badly, but still not getting what you want, which hurts them even more. This is like the proverbial football dad, who is trying to live his own dream through his son. It is unhealthy for the father but completely devastating to the son.

Say your two-year-old son is defiant. Imagine he looks a consequence—you—in the face and laughs. You should see virtue in that sin. He has a personality that has the potential for facing good conflict and not running. He also has the potential for being disobedient to godly authority—as you just discovered. It is the parent's duty to take this raw product and shape it with discipline until it is a virtue and not a vice.

We have a daughter who loves to be involved. Even at a very little age we could tell that she didn't have a lot of discernment about what to join in on. She would toddle along with her older sister's discipline and ask to have spankings too—just to be part of the fun. As time has gone by we have seen more of that from her, and we love it. She is a dynamite playmate. She jumps into almost anything whole hog. But obviously she needs to learn to discern what she gets involved with in the first place. Being a lively participant in bad behavior is only a shade away from being the most outspoken objector. She has what it takes to make things happen and to get people involved—it is our job to see that she knows how to use that wisely.

Another little girl I know has tremendous power to please people. She just knows what people want. Her parents very wisely talk to her about being the kind of person who can either use that to bless the people around her or to manipulate them. It is two sides of the same coin, and they have been wise enough to see both sides of it and make her see it too.

What I am trying to get at is that you do not want to discipline vices as though they are unconnected to virtues. They are almost always the good and the bad manifestations of the same thing. When you see a vice manifesting in your child, take the time to think through how you *do* want them to use it. Is your daughter being catty and critical of another child's artwork? Tell her how you want to hear her using her tongue to build up. Teach her how to encourage. Make her practice while you listen, and encourage her with smiles, winks, or nods.

But there is another temptation that is almost more damaging. Often, parents will notice a virtue and then preen that virtue to the point that it becomes a vice. Having established in their minds that this virtue (whatever it is) is a good thing, they quit thinking critically about it or noticing it, often because they now share a blind spot with that child.

What started out as a tender conscience quickly deteriorated into a self-righteous little girl that no one but the parents thinks is cute. What originally manifested itself as a cheerful heart and a sweet voice became almost overnight a parent-pleasing, self-consumed diva. None of the siblings enjoy the concerts, because they all see the superiority complex and not so much the giftedness. The parents continue on, sometimes for the entire length of their daughter's childhood, favoring a vice.

I once read advice for opening a bed and breakfast that seemed very wise. Spend a night in each room. Find out if there is a cold breeze coming from that window and what the beds are like. By spending the night in it, you might find out that you don't have enough pillows or some such easily corrected problem. Now of course you can't actually do this with your children, but what you can do is the thought experiment.

Imagine yourself as one of your children. Try to really examine what life for them is like. Be honest. Are you the kid who always has to give away a toy because your younger brother will scream and you won't? Are you the kid who wants to paint more than anything in the world but your mom doesn't want the mess? Are you the biggest kid who has to clean up for the little ones all the time? Are you the kid who stands with your mom while she complains about you to strangers in the grocery store? Do you only ever get to wear hand-me-downs? Are you the oldest daughter who wants to be playing with a friend, but is instead making freezer meals to lay up for the next twelve years? Are you the little girl who has to sit through dinner every night listening to your older sister impress the parents with her sparkling abilities? Do you feel lonely, left out, ignored? Could you sum up your role in the family as "free babysitter"? Do you have any reason to feel like your parents are not interested in you? Have you heard them sharing your failings with people that you don't know? Embarrassing moments? Do your parents compare you to your sister? Are your talents, your looks, or your personality held up in light of hers? Do your parents seem to only give you token hugs?

What is life really like for your kids? You might really be surprised at what you see by simply taking a minute to look. And if you notice that your child's life is cold and drafty and lacking in pillows, you had better make some changes.

CHAPTER FOURTEEN

Growth Spurts

One of the most difficult things my children can do is grow. And they just keep doing it, don't they? It seems like we just find a routine and things are fairly manageable. I am feeling pretty good about the laundry, about the discipline, and about the whole situation. Then it seems like we wake up one morning and nothing works anymore. The twins are spending the days having intellectual disagreements that are very hard to sort through. The big girls are listless, bored, and usually demanding a lot more of something, like talking or concentrated play, or they are just begging me for something "special" to do. Usually a project. I don't know what they are talking about—being caught up on the laundry is special enough for me!

This is a feeling that almost always accompanies some kind of change: someone giving up the need for a nap, someone learning to run, someone finding out they can climb up on to the table, the big girls discovering they can tie things together, or what have you. Anyway, this can be very frustrating. The kids may be alternately bouncing off the wall and fussing with each other, or getting into things you don't want them doing, or demanding something of you that you were not prepared to give.

Whenever this happens, this ambiguous restlessness in the house, I try to think of it as a growth spurt. It is like all my children have a growth spurt at the same time and develop new needs. This is only a problem when Mom doesn't have a growth spurt herself. It's even more of a problem when Mom refuses to have one, and demands that everyone else get back into clothes that are too tight. Just like the wine and the wineskins, you can't make the old schedule work with the new needs. Naps, when filled with children who no longer need them, crack open and make a big mess.

Once again, I find that the children's attitudes are tethered to mine. If I pray for a growth spurt, for ideas on how to help them, how to make this a fun new phase, and how to appreciate their new needs, then the change on my part usually clears up a lot of things. I am not saying that this eliminates the need for discipline, but it makes it gloriously clear-cut and sweet. My attitude is no longer a player, and it is no longer a big "situation." It is just normal life.

You know those pain scales at the hospital, where they rate your pain from one to ten? Well, pretend that you are screaming, "Thirteen, thirteen! Fifteen!" What that should tell you is that it is time to restart the whole thing, stop screaming, and just deal with the fact that this is now the new "one." Start over, and accept the new "normal."

I promise that this little mental change will actually change how you feel, and by extension how your children feel.

Growing is, after all, what God wants them to do.

CHAPTER FIFTEEN

I Am a Racquetball Court

Here is a little mental image that may be helpful for those of you who have little dinks like I do. I like to think of them as a bunch of little racquetball players, and I am the court. Only in this version of the game, my job is to make the walls big shock absorbers. They throw things at my walls, or hit them, or otherwise propel them at me, and it is my job to absorb the shock. I must take a bad attitude with a lot of spin and turn it into a quiet little ball rolling across the floor. Sometimes it seems like we can get caught up in the game— "You throw that backtalk at me, buster, and it's gonna come back at you so fast you're gonna need protective eye gear"—just to take an example.

This thought is especially helpful for me when all the kiddos are cruising at once. Sometimes it is just a little crazy. I try to think about my own walls. How can I insulate these? How can I be one big muffle for all the fussiness? Can I change the subject? Could we go on a big explore to stomp on chestnuts? Could I just put away the dolls of discord and yell, "Time for a popcorn party!"

Of course the most important step in all this is to pray for grace and repent of any racquetball throwing of your own. But as every busy mother knows, it's not like you can just walk away from the great PBJ debacle to go have a quiet time. In my own experience, it usually amounts to a quick prayer of "Lord, help me absorb" while still in the midst of whatever it was that happened with the coffee grounds.

A very important part of this for me is that my job is not to contain the explosions, it is to end them. When our kids are having trouble fighting about something, we go change the subject. Of course we deal with any outstanding sin, but the attitude can be trickier. It is not about ignoring the sin, it is about renewing the fellowship.

When I think about my children growing up, I often think about the character that I want to be in their lives. When I have a teenage daughter who is worked up about some problem with a classmate and comes to talk to me, I want her to go away calm. I don't want to jump on her for any traces of sin that I may see in her attitude; I want to help her abandon them.

So, there it is for what it's worth, and maybe, just maybe, it will come to mind and help you the next time you find the kids playing in the Crisco.

CHAPTER SIXTEEN

Grabby Hearts & Grabby Hands

When our children are fussing with each other (say they both want a flashlight—very possible), we will interrupt them and ask them a few questions. First of all we ask them to tell us what they did that was wrong, leaving the other person out of the narrative. We will probably spend a minute sorting through the blow by blow, and then ask "What is more important—this flashlight, or your sister?" After they answer (and believe it or not they do know the answer), we will ask them what they were pretending was more important. They know that too. So we tell them to get it right.

They need to apologize to each other for breaking fellowship over a flashlight. I like for them to say that because it makes it perfectly clear to them what exchange they were making. Flashlight for sister. This is not a complex "who had it for how long" situation. It is not our job to run in and settle the dispute as though it were an honest and legitimate dispute. Flashlights are not to come between us in fellowship. Ever.

This is not to say that we don't do a fair bit of negotiating. We do, because at the end of the day the flashlight has to end up somewhere, but what we are working on is giving them the tools to figure it out amongst themselves. Once they are back in fellowship, we can talk about flashlight details. If there was a scuffle, both are in the wrong. If only one member of the flashlight grabbers was in the wrong, the other would have come found me to ask for help. If what I hear is two voices raised together in fury, everyone is wrong, regardless of who first grabbed. There is a wrong way to be right and a wrong way to be wrong.

We might talk about ideas for sharing the flashlight, polite ways of responding, but I like to have them try it again. Keep in mind that at this point they may have been spanked if the fuss was bad enough, or they may have just apologized. Either way, they are back in fellowship. I will ask them to have the whole exchange again, responding like Christians, and staying in fellowship. While this doesn't always go perfectly, they do a pretty good job of it.

If the children continue under the thrall of the flashlight and are unable to deal with each other kindly so long as it is in the room, I will talk to them about getting rid of it. Cheerfully, and in a "let's brainstorm here to deal with our trouble" kind of way. It is hilarious how this clears the mind for them. It would be better to throw away the flashlight and stay in fellowship with your sister. Suddenly it seems that they have found a second wind. They can work it out after all. Just as Bree in C. S. Lewis's *The Horse and His Boy* could run faster with the threat of a lion behind him, so our children find that, with the threat of the garbage looming, they can share after all.

Now the point of this is not to rush to the "I will throw away all the toys if you ever fuss again" kind of moment. And none of it should be spoken through your teeth with your lips not even moving. And it shouldn't be a bluff or a threat, and you are not offering to throw it away out of spite. The point of it is to show your children that you value their relationship to each other, and expect them to also. If there is something that is getting between them, we need to fix that, one way or another. Make it clear to them that you want to see it change in their hearts. Grabby hands come from grabby hearts.

Once I picked up one of those Fisher-Price plastic coupe cars at a rummage sale. If ever there was a vehicle for sin, this was it. After about thirty minutes of ownership, we began calling it the "sin wagon." We muscled through a lot of drama about that thing. It even had the same magical effect on visiting children. Shoving, screaming, pushing, camping out in the driver's seat for an eternity smirking at the line of people waiting, pushing it wildly around the room with someone screaming inside. My husband said it was like a permanent balloon. We sold it at our yard sale—I hoped it was an only child who got it. I don't think that the verse about causing little ones to stumble was directly talking about plastic coupe cars, but it was at the very least a veiled allusion.

Of course sharing is one of the biggest issues of a child's life—what they have to share, whom they have to share it with, who has to share what with them, and all the many nuances that each of those entail. When you have a bunch of kids close in age, many of the toys end up being communal, and occasional conflict is par for the course. Remember that the house rules for the toys are foundational social laws to your child. They will take these lessons with them for life. So think through what your rules communicate to your children.

Do your kids know that if they grab the toy they want and cry, Mom will make their brother give it to them in a minute? Do you try to pacify them by offering them things and trying to persuade them that it is better, rather than just deal with the envy? Do you let them live their life with a sidelong glance—always wanting what someone else has and finding a way to get it?

At our house we try to avoid super hard and fast rules because they tend to create legalists out of all of us. Your kids can be caught up in the middle of a toy snatch-off ("It's mine! I had it first!") only to have Mom come sailing in for the winning snatch ("Give that to me, you two stinkers!"). Grabby hearts make grabby hands. It is the hearts that are the problem. Only sorting out what they may grab and when does not deal with the actual situation because it does not address the engine of the situation—their hearts. Nobody profits from this kind of system, but everyone learns how to work it to their advantage.

It is important to stick to principles, teach principles, and then sort out the details in light of them. You need to look at what you think is happening in hearts and address that.

Generally at our house you have to ask to play with something that belongs to someone else, and generally they have to let you (if they aren't currently using it, and if it isn't brand new, super-special, or something you are likely to break).

You may always politely ask to have something that someone else has, and they may politely decline. If they do, you may not cry about it. You may ask to have it whenever they are finished. You will then need to vacate the area, not hover and complain that it is taking too long.

If you are playing with something that belongs to a sibling, and they ask for it back, you must give it. But if you are the owner, you may not go around seizing your toys as soon as you notice anyone else enjoying them, just because they are enjoying it.

You cannot hoard toys like a dragon hoards treasure, alone and in a cave. Our children have even gone so far as to physically lie down on a toy—the perfect picture of a dragon. So you may not be a dragon—that is a hard and fast rule.

Now every time your children have a conflict about a toy, they are breaking fellowship. If you step in and redistribute the toy but don't address the unkindness or selfishness or envy, you allow that to stay between them. It is sort of like trying to get rid of a dandelion by shaking the seeds all over your garden. There we go. Solved that problem. Until later this afternoon.

It is a lot harder to work through the grabby heart problems than the grabby hands, even though they usually travel together. If this part of parenting were only about toy distribution, then we should just be setting timers and keeping tally sheets. But teaching them about dealing well with each other, looking to their own hearts, and staying in fellowship is hugely important if they are ever going to get on without you. If you take the time to train them in this, you will find yourself needing to negotiate less and less. When conflict arises, as it will, you will have less to talk about because they will recognize the real problem and be able to get the fellowship restored as quickly as they broke it.

CHAPTER SEVENTEEN

A Gracious Law

Obviously a huge part of mothering little people is discipline. It is certainly not all you do, but it is very central. Your children are getting acquainted with the world God made, and they have to learn the boundaries. God put you in their lives to help with this.

The first stage of discipline is all about establishing your authority. Mama said, "No touch." Baby touched, so who's in charge here? Now even at this early stage, you need to make sure that what you are teaching is that your authority over them comes from God, and God is in authority over the both of you together.

As your children get older and they begin to have more complex discipline needs, this structure needs to stay firmly in place. You discipline because you are the rightful authority over them, and the rightful authority over the both of you is God. You need to be pointing them to His law as you explain yours. God said, "Love your neighbor as yourself," so Mama says, "You may not hit one another."

If you do not maintain your authority, but start grabbing for power and control, you will end up simply being an electric dog collar to your children. Aside from your little exertions of power, they can see no reason why they should still be in the backyard. You may successfully limit their activities to the area you set out, but they will not have embraced the boundaries. Take this a little further down the road—what happens when they leave your house? Will they be up in the neighbor's chicken coop in a heartbeat? Maybe all the shocks from the collar just led them to believe that life everywhere is pointless and not worth pursuing, but that is still not a disciplinary success. If the dog stays on the porch forever without any particular loyalty to it, you have a different kind of problem and a boring one too.

There is a very important distinction between authority and power. Your authority should always be geared toward guiding with an eye toward releasing. Authority into freedom. One of the things that I love about sending our children to school (a wonderful Christian school) is that we are giving them the responsibility for their behavior. We are saying, "You know how to obey your teacher, and you know how we want you to act on the playground—so go do it! Tell me how it goes." Of course we still closely watch how they are doing, but they know full well that we are trusting them to do the right thing, and that it is their responsibility and privilege.

Power never wants to let go, and always grabs for more. An example might be if your child goes off and misbehaves at a friend's house, so you respond with a power grab. "You can't have a snack now. I won't let you play your Nintendo now. Now you can't have a friend over." Discipline like this is about control and not authority. This is why you see parents who start cracking down harder and harder as their kids get older and older. If you are disciplining in a power regime, you will find that if you give an inch, they take a mile. Give your daughter money to go shopping, and she will come home with things you would never have bought. Give your son the keys to the car, and he will prove to you what a bad idea that was. This is because every little gap in your power is like a hole in the electric fence, offering them a chance at freedom. This might leave the parents with the impression that they ought to tighten up, but what they should have done was loosen up a long time ago. As our children grow, we ought to be releasing them from our authority to God's authority alongside us.

I can still remember when my dad told us (I think in late high school) that we were free to watch any movie we wanted. It did not cause a rash of inappropriate movie watching among us. I think if anything, it made him more involved in our movie watching. Instead of calling to ask if we could watch a movie at a party, we were walking out of movies at parties and talking to him in great detail about it afterwards. He had put in the time with us, teaching us to love the standards. We would watch music videos with him while he picked apart the worldview propaganda they promoted. So when he released us to our own entertainment standards, we already knew we were expected to be discerning, and we took it as a real responsibility. Because of this, we were constantly asking for help, talking through things, and checking in on what he thought of what we were watching.

If your children are as young as mine, then we are not quite at that parenting level yet. But we are laying the foundation. Keep an eye on the time when they will be free of your law—you want them to have learned to love God's. So explain your decisions, and always be open for their sincere questions. As popular as it is, "Because I said so" is usually not the best explanation.

I try to remember that my relationship with my children will be, Lord willing, one of friendship far longer than it is one of authority. This phase where we wield the rod is a short one. As they grow up and our authority is released, it should be releasing our relationship to friendship in that area.

The best way to be sure of this is to emphasize fellowship: fellowship with one another and with God. When you have disciplined, there should be a restoration of fellowship. There is not a time when you should discipline with a break in fellowship—you should never spend time being "mad" at a child. If it is broken, restore it. Scripture says that if we walk in the light as

He is in the light, we have fellowship with one another (1 Jn. 1:7). You cannot discipline a child for being out of fellowship if you also are out of fellowship.

This is all another way of saying that the entire goal of disciplining your children is to bring them up to walk in the light with you. Teach them what it looks like to live under authority by the way that you live under God's. When you sin against your children, make it right. Do not think that apologizing for being harsh will make you look like you shouldn't be in charge. They saw the sin; they need to see you make it right. It is an example to them of how to live under authority.

CHAPTER EIGHTEEN

No Need to Count

If you have a baby, chances are pretty good that you are up a lot in the night, or at least have a fair bit of interrupted sleep. My sister-in-law passed on a piece of advice to me that I think has some real wisdom. Get rid of your clock, at least the one you can see when your eyes are rolling around in your head while you nurse. You don't need to know what time it is until it is morning. If the baby is awake, so are you. I think it is quite easy for mothers to be tallying up their awake moments in the night so they can be certain just how much they gave. "I was up for thirty-five minutes at 3:00 a.m., and then he woke up at 4:00 a.m. for another forty minutes! So basically, I didn't sleep at all last night." Honestly though, who really needed to know how much they were up? You were just up when you needed to be.

God gave us two great sleepers in our first two girls. They were up in the night like all babies, but it was pretty reasonable. That is why it was so funny when the twins came along. They were individually probably average babies; together—an all-night-long circus. While we were already seasoned parents, we were not prepared for anything like this! They were born right around midnight. I decided to try to get a little sleep around 2:30 a.m. or something, so I sent them out for the nurses to watch. I can still remember the feeling—through the door about every hour would come this rolling bassinet with two screaming infants in it. It was totally outrageous. I remember wondering how this could possibly be my problem right now? What am I supposed to do with two of them? We muddled our way through all right, but that was a good picture of what it was going to be like having twins.

Tricky things would happen in the night. Sometimes (okay, almost all the time) Titus would wake up nicely swaddled in a pink blanket and Chloe in the red one. To be fair to us, more often than not we would wake up to find that we had tucked some diapers into our bed, so it wasn't just Titus who felt the brunt of our sleeplessness.

The highest of low points for us happened one night a few months in. When the babies would wake up to nurse, Luke would get them for me, and I would sit up in bed and nurse them. He would change the diapers and burp them at intervals. (It is worth a detour to note that there were a lot of diapers. It seemed quite often that we knew that someone had done it, but it was not clear who, and Luke would try to ascertain that critical piece of information while I chipped in with clues. No sooner would he have cleared up the situation but one of them would fire off again, and we would be back to square one. If there is one thing we know about newborns, it is that there is no real method to the madness.)

In this way, we could cruise through between four and six diapers at a feeding, in the dead of the night. I would sleep with my head dangling off to the side, because no matter how you slice it, you can't nurse two babies while sleeping in any natural position. So this is how it would go. Eventually I would wake back up with my arms asleep and neck hurting and two infants conked out on top of me.

So one night we had followed the routine up to this point, when I woke with a start and the feeling of desperation. I needed to lie down; I needed to set these babies down. But I also needed them to stay sleeping. So I tried to wake Luke up. Nothing. Since leaping out of bed gracefully with two sleeping infants (who were propped up on pillows) and then somehow gently getting them into the crib with one arm apiece was out of the question, I kept trying to wake him up.

I started kicking. Just a nice quick toe-punch to the shins. I wouldn't say *nothing* happened, but it wasn't much. After a lot of kicking and sort of sharp whispering, he sat up. I was relieved. But it was premature. He didn't do anything. Slowly, he got out of bed and turned to lean on it. Then, after a minute or two, he gathered himself up and headed out of the room. I don't think I need to tell you that I was firing off lots of urgent questions at this sudden development, but he was on a mission and couldn't stop to talk.

After a bit of frustration and an effort at moving the kiddos myself, I bit the bullet and waited. Presumably he had decided to use the facilities before helping his wife out. I was annoyed in that middle-of-the-night kind of way. After a few minutes he reappeared in the door but passed the room by.

At this point I was pretty much whisper-shouting, which is hard to do, but if you practice you can get it. He passed by the door again and I saw it—he was bouncing a baby. Patting it on its little air back and soothing it back to sleep. He was being the most selfless and kind daddy, walking the hall in the middle of the night with his dream baby. I hate to admit how totally unamused I was. I was frantically whisper-shouting, "Stop it! Stop it! *You* do not have a baby—I have the babies! Wake up! Wake up! Get the babies! *That is not a baby!* WAKE UP! YOU ARE NOT HOLDING A BABY! I HAVE THE BABIES, BOTH OF THEM, AND YOU MUST WAKE UP AND TAKE THEM! WAKE UP! LUUUUUUUUKE!"

Eventually he did wake up and just came and took them and sweetly tucked them in as though nothing had happened at all. And you know, I think I was asleep again before he had even finished laying them down. We had a really good laugh about it in the morning (when I was not at all annoyed), and it is now one of our fondest memories of the early days with the twins—a sort of high point of sleeplessness.

CHAPTER NINETEEN

Expectations

One of the greatest kindnesses you can do for your kids is to lay out for them clear expectations. Think ahead a minute, explain what is going to happen. When it does happen, what do you want to see them doing? It is easy for parents to start dealing with little kids like they are a bunch of boxes you are carrying around, and the more you shift positions the less stable your grip becomes. They are actually capable of doing a lot more than you might think, but only if you make your expectations perfectly clear.

When the twins were born, we developed a stroller walking system for the bigger girls. Realizing that there was absolutely no way that I could catch them both if they to decided to take off, I knew that we had to make some pretty firm rules. I had two cord-like things attached to the stroller—we called them the stations. They were responsible to hold onto their stations while we walked. This kept them right beside me, our pace pretty good, and I could see right away if they let go, and if they did they were still right beside me.

It also made going on walks a total pleasure. Instead of spending the whole time saying, "Come on. Hurry up. Slow down. Stop there. Wait a minute," we would talk about other things—the plants we saw, the dreams they had, and all the rest. A minute or two into our walk (usually as we approached the first major street crossing), I would ask, "What's the big, big rule?" and they would respond with, "Do not let go of *stations!*"

After we had done enough station walking to know they were capable, I took them to the mall with me for a practice run. If you have your hands full of little people, I really recommend this. I had no reason to go to the mall. I did not need to look for anything, I was not going to try on clothes or anything. In other words, we went to the mall exclusively to practice our behavior.

We would have a little talk, and I would tell them, "We are going to go into this store. There are a lot of breakable things in here—so, I want you to hold on to your station, and when I tell you to, put your other hand in your pocket. Talk about what you see, don't touch." We would make a loop through the store and come out. If they had done a good job, I would be ecstatic. I would kneel down so that we could talk face to face, and I would be super-positive and encouraging. If we weren't so great—if a hand had jumped from a pocket to touch something, we would talk about it and try again. Not a huge deal, but we can do better. This is teamwork, and it takes work from all of us. Sometimes we would practice not holding on—being allowed to walk up ahead of me. The big point of this exercise was to come back right away if I called them. They loved knowing exactly what I wanted them to do and then excelling at it.

A very important aspect of this kind of training is that it should occur when it doesn't matter very much. Do not try to train your kids in the security line at the airport. No one should be stressed out or currently disobeying, and the outcome should not be a life or death situation. You should practice for fun. If you have done this before, then your children will not even notice when the stakes are high on their obedience.

The other thing is that the structure is a fence—around freedom. We go on fun walks to practice our obeying and end up at the park, where we run around and play for a while. Obedience to God's law is freedom. Your kids should feel the same way about obeying you. Sometimes you should give them little jobs to obey, knowing full well that they will love to do it. Praise them for their quick obeying. You should not be training them that obedience is bondage. Do not do epic training camps that teach them that obedience leads to sitting quietly on your hands and speaking to no one. Obedience to Scripture is life. So if you are giving lots of commands it should be things like, "Okay, stir this. Grab the eggs out of the fridge. Great. Dump in the flour. Nice job." God does not command things that make life miserable—His commands are a means of joy. Make your children understand that obedience leads to freedom and joy—it is the path of life.

Sometimes you have a situation where the kids act like a bunch of BBs, and you start stressing out. Did you ever talk to them about what is supposed to happen? Have you made it clear what you want them to do, or are you just annoyed at what they do to fill the moment? My husband has actually organized the kids' formations: Alpha, Bravo, and Charlie. They love the importance of it, it cracks Daddy up (as well as everyone who sees us, I think), and they have fun with it. Instead of Mom or Dad trying to micromanage who stands where, it is a way of saying, "Okay kids, you know what to do! Go!" It also keeps us from spending the whole time barking out little commands, and frees us to talk to them and praise the good work they are doing.

Making expectations clear is hugely important. So is making them reasonable. Do not micromanage their lives. As a general rule of thumb, you should use this sort of tool as a way of decreasing the bossiness, not increasing. If you have a situation in life where you are constantly firing off commands, it is a good idea to see if there is a way of streamlining it. As my parents always said, the garden was full of trees to eat from, and only one was a "no touch." Structure and freedom combined together make happy children. Too much of either is very destructive.

Yesterday was cold and dark and rainy and so were my little people. We were having the kind of morning where the kids lie sort of draped on the edge of things and claim to be physically unable to take off their pj's. Lots of weak knees and hair in our eyes. It was time for me to clear out the commands (Put your pants on! Stand up!) and increase the freedom (I've got a good idea!). This was not a good time for parental demands.

So here's what we did (don't get me wrong—you could do this without bad attitudes first). I just helped them get dressed with a lot of excitement, and I made them put on their sneakers because they were going to show me some of their "crazy skills." Then, we made the crash pile. It consisted of several couch pillows, two down comforters, an afghan, and a lot of miscellany. I showed them the route that I wanted them to run—start at the end of the hall, through the dining room, into the living room, and then the crash pile! We set up a drink station at the end of the hall to be refreshed between runs! I'm sure all of you moms know what happened—rosy cheeks, lots of hilarity, some of the craziest skills you've ever seen—all the good stuff! When we got tired of running, we pulled chairs over to it and jumped high into the air into the crash pile.

We try to make our expectations perfectly clear to our children, and most of the time we expect them to just have fun and enjoy themselves.

CHAPTER TWENTY

A Good Word

Sometime when I was pregnant with the twins I remember that I was having a lot of trouble getting to mopping the floor in the living room. There was one very provocative sticky spot that had been weighing on me for days. Yes, days. I would clean everything to prepare to mop it, and then be interrupted for dinner or something. There was also an entire graham cracker that lived under our buffet for weeks because I could only see it from a special angle I had when collapsed on the couch.

Finally I managed it. I felt so liberated and victorious. I had gotten the kids out of the room for long enough when the room was clean enough to actually mop. Success. Empowerment.

The next day I woke up and discovered a new sticky spot—magically created overnight by who knows what. Of course everything was now back to the way it had been, and I felt suddenly completely defeated. That sticky floor came out at me like a rude taunt: "You will never win!" I remember thinking that if I recalled correctly there was an entire book of the Bible devoted to this kind of situation. I went off to read Ecclesiastes until I found something that really put a finger on it.

"Everyone to whom God has given wealth, and possessions, and the power to enjoy them, and to accept his lot and rejoice in his toil—this is the gift of God. For he will not much remember the days of his life because God keeps him occupied with joy in his heart" (Eccl. 5:19).

Blessings, like children, are not ethereal and weightless. Sometimes they feel like they come at you like a Kansas hail storm—they might leave a welt! But if you accept your lot and rejoice in your toil, God will give you the kind of overwhelming joy that cannot remember the details. Motherhood is hard work. It is repetitive and often times menial. Accept it. Rejoice in it. This is your toil. Right here. Those are their faces. Enjoy them. The days of your life are supposed to be full of things like this. But joy is not giddy. It is not an emotional rush—it is what happens when you accept your lot and rejoice in your toil. So rejoice in your children. Look them in the eyes and give thanks. You will not even remember the work of all this planting when the harvest of joy overwhelms you.